The
Big Book
of
Camping Hacks,
Hints, and Help

Gia Scott

DEDICATION

For my mom, the first one to take me camping.
For my grandmother, who taught me a lot.
For my kids, who taught me to slow down and have fun.
For my husband, who tolerates my eccentricity

Table of Contents

What are camping hacks, hints, and help anyhow?

Camping hacks are hints and ideas to make the camp trip easier, safer, cheaper, and/or more fun. Not every hack or hint is a great idea for every camper, but almost everyone should find a lot of ideas to make their camping trip easier, safer, cheaper, and more fun.

Don't wait to go through these hacks until you are on your camping trip either! They work best if you know far in advance of your trip how to use a particular hack or hint, and plan your trip to include it. Other hacks or hints may be put into use during your trip to keep it safer, healthier, or neater. Whichever the case, read them through several times, thinking about which ones will work the best for your family and your situation. Some are for car campers, others are for backpackers, some work for use even at home!

How to use this book

Knowing what is in the book is a critical part of the process, and that means reading it and then re-reading it again. Share it with the other family members so that everyone has an opportunity to know what is in the book. Take a copy, either digital or print, along on your trip—it just might come in handy!

The book is divided according to topic, so for hints about how to manage your camp fire, you would look under camp fire. That means you would also find things about roasting over the camp fire under camp fire. For finding out how to clean the soot off of your pots and pans from using them on your camp stove or camp fire, you would look under cleaning. Understanding what is in each section will make referring to the book for specific hacks, hints and help much easier.

Activities

Not everyone is content with pitching a tent and then lounging in its vicinity for days on end. To entertain the more energetic crowd, plan activities during the camping excursion.

Evenings in camp can include card games. A deck of cards is small, compact, and lightweight, which makes them a candidate for going along even on a backpacking trip.

Other compact games that can be enjoyed while camping include dominoes and Yahtzee (or other dice games). Dominoes are great while camping in breezy weather, as they stay put on the table.

Campfire sing a longs are a long tradition. Bring along the lyrics for several songs to help jog your memory. Just remember, not everyone appreciates a late night serenade session, so in a campground, call it over before quiet time.

Plan a "treasure hunt" for the kids to encourage their interest in the nature that is surrounding them on a camping trip. Make a checklist of things for them to find nearby or while participating in a nature walk or hike. Remember, look but don't touch! Leave the flowers, plants, rocks, and other things where they are. Don't forget to add a "prize" to the event, which can be anything from a special treat to being able to choose the next family activity.

Participate in park programs. Many parks will offer a variety of activities, especially in summer and on weekends. Find out what is offered and join in. Usually, there is also no extra fee for participating.

Many parks offer great cycling opportunities. Bring along the bicycles for the entire family and take advantage of them.

Be safe with all activities. Follow posted rules in designated recreation areas.

Putting life preservers on toddlers and preschoolers when participating in activities near water can add peace of mind. Falls into the water are inevitable for bolder children who are intent on exploring, and the life preserver can help if it is deep water.

Renting a boat or a canoe can help create memories that everyone will cherish, even if no one is an expert with the boat or canoe. Boat rentals are often located in popular recreation areas.

Simple games such as catch or flying disks can be entertaining and fun.

Bring along cards, coloring books, or reading books for rainy day activities inside the tent.

Observe other campers and see if you pick up on any ideas for great camping activities. Use the opportunity to learn from others, and even asking other parents about things they do with their kids can lead to truly great ideas.

Try group camping with a few other families. By sharing equipment, ideas, and skills, everyone ends up having even more fun than they would on their own.

Join a camping club. Experienced campers are not all created equal, and learning from others is possible at any stage of the game. Discussions, demonstrations, and events are all great times to expand your own skills and come up with new ideas to make camping fun.

Many clubs are loosely organized and do not even charge dues, while others are more regimented in their organization. If the group doesn't fit, feel free to leave it and try another.

Join hiking or bird watching clubs. Group events can often be very educational as well as fun. Learning from others happens even with experienced hikers and bird watchers. It also encourages networking and social interaction with others with shared interests.

Alcohol

Many parks ban all alcoholic beverages. Others only ban glass containers. Find out before you arrive with a forbidden item.

DIY Sangria—fill a large jar with mixed fresh fruit, including grapes. Fill the jar about ¼ full with vodka, then add wine of your choice to completely fill the jar. Stash it in your cooler, and you've got your own sangria!

Grown up roasted marshmallows—pour some Irish Cream liquor into a glass or mug. Dip freshly roasted marshmallows into the liquor and indulge your inner child too. Try other sweet liquors such as Kahlua or crème de menthe for variety too.

No ice? Chill your beer or wine by immersing it in a cold running stream near your campsite. Just make sure your stash isn't raided by underage raiders!

Backpacks, Daypacks, fanny packs and lumbar packs

There are entire books devoted to the details and arts involved with backpacks and backpacking. This isn't one, and is not going to pretend that it is. This description is to help the novices understand some of the choices that are available.

Backpacks are found in two basic types: internal frame and external frame.

Internal frame backpacks were originally designed for rock climbing and other types of hiking and climbing that required a narrower, more streamlined pack. Today, they are the most common type and are the least expensive of the two. Sizes vary, and those considering an extensive backpacking trip would be well advised to have an experienced backpacker assist them in choosing one that is appropriately sized to their body and the anticipated load.

External backpacks are a type of pack that is attached to a framework. Today, that framework is apt to be of a lightweight metal alloy. These packs can carry more weight and have more flexibility in what they are carrying than an internal frame pack does by the existence of the frame itself, which allows for attachments of all kinds of gear and pack options. Once again, for proper fit, one should consult an experienced backpacker.

Day packs are the run of the mill frameless pack designed to carry a lightweight load for a single day. These are also commonly used for carrying books to school, laptops, commuting, etc. and are available in very inexpensive models. They allow a hiker to carry a few emergency supplies, a snack or meal, a rain poncho or rain coat, and water for a day's outing. Day packs are also manufactured to fit young children, allowing them to carry their own drinks, snacks, and toys whether it is on a hike or to the beach.

Fanny packs refer to the inexpensive pouches-on-a-belt that are sold in a variety of outlets. Many women use them as an alternative to a purse, and men often use them as well. They are made out of a variety of materials, including ripstop nylon and leather, and come in an equal variety of color schemes. Some also have a holster to hold one or two water bottles. They are typically held around the waist with a plastic quick connect clip on a nylon strap for a belt and are adjustable to fit most people.

Lumbar packs are nearly identical to fanny packs but are a higher tech version capable of more weight and with a larger capacity, along with a higher price tag. They ride low on the back, and some come with one or two shoulder straps to help distribute the weight as well. Look at the different models before choosing the one that you think will suit you best.

Why use any of these unless you are backpacking? They offer convenient packing and easy carrying to and from your car. Day packs are great for a day outing, whether camping or at home, as they will carry everything you may need. Lumbar and fanny packs are great on excursions, as they hold your essentials such as money, keys, wallet, and camera while leaving your hands free.

Bathing and Personal Hygiene

Many campgrounds offer hot showers for no additional fee, along with sinks and flush toilets. In these campgrounds, the most difficult part of the personal hygiene routine is to not leave items behind. To minimize loss, use sample or travel size products when possible.

Bring along the wet wipes, especially when primitive camping when showers are impossible or difficult.

No camp shower? Buy a new sprayer from a garden center, such as is used for insecticides, with the pump up container. Fill with warm water and shower away! The water flow is adjustable too.

Use no rinse soap/shampoo, such as used in hospitals, when water use is being kept to a minimum. Even rinsing it out of hair and off of skin is easier than with regular soaps and shampoos, and it leaves the hair soft and clean too.

Hand sanitizers can really help with keeping clean when water is scarce. Small bottles also pack into backpacks easily.

Go unscented. Scented products, from shampoos to deodorants, can attract insects. Perfumes may contain ingredients that attract animals as well. Leave them at home and enjoy nature's own scents.

Skip the curling iron and hair gel when camping. It's not necessary, even if it does amuse people to see others insisting on using them.

Bring toilet paper. Keep it dry in a recycled coffee can or CD spindle. Even with restrooms, campgrounds often run out of toilet paper. In primitive campsites without a bathroom, do not litter the ground with used toilet paper—it takes years to decompose and is simply gross to look at. Bag it and pack it out or burn it in your campfire, just not while you are cooking!

Bears

Bear populations are rising, and as a result, they are coming into contact with people more often. Despite their cute and cuddly appearance, they are a very large predator that sometimes has a very bad temper. Do not feed the bears.

Many campgrounds and national parks require that all food items be secured in a bear proof canister. These canisters can be rented or purchased.

Trash cans in bear country are designed to reduce scavenging by bears. Use them properly to dispose of waste.

Remember, used dishes and pots must also be stored in a bear proof container.

Many bears have learned how to gain access to vehicles to seek food as well. Unfortunately, they are not particularly concerned about damaging the vehicle when they do so.

For personal protection against bears, bear spray is recommended. This is a high powered, large dose of pepper spray designed to actually deter a bear. Regular pepper sprays are regarded as mere seasoning by bears.

Many bears have learned how to defeat the hanging bag that was used to prevent bears from accessing food in the past and it is no longer a recommended method of protecting food from bears.

Beds and Bedding

In cold weather, insulate yourself from the cold ground. This means using a sleeping pad or multiple layers, as just a sleeping bag will not be enough. Piling dry leaves on the ground before setting up your tent can help cushion the interior as well as provide additional insulation from the ground.

A rolled up jacket or other clothing can make a great pillow. This reduces the amount of overall gear required to stay comfortable while camping.

In cold weather, tuck your clothing in the bottom of the sleeping bag. It will be warm the next morning when you put it on, and it will help keep you warmer during the night.

Hate the cold? Add one or two microfleece throws to your bedroll for snuggly warmth in bed. Use one as a shawl or wrap to stay warm around the campfire too. Adding the microfleece can also help an aging sleeping bag retain warmth better.

Got a new baby and no portable crib? Use a laundry

basket padded with a folded blanket or towel as a portable crib for the very young set, and drape with mosquito netting to keep the insects at bay too. This only works with very young babies, about 0-4 months.

100% wool blankets are heavy, but they retain their ability to keep you warm even when wet. They are an excellent addition to a sleeping bag in cold, damp weather.

Don't store sleeping bags in their compression sacks (that's the small sack it came in) as it will also compress their insulation until they are not nearly as warm as they once were. Instead, hang them in a closet if possible, or store loosely rolled in a larger bag, like an old pillow case.

Wash sleeping bags in large capacity front loading machines, not in the average top loading home washer, even if it means making a trip to the Laundromat. Wash 1 or 2 bags, depending on size, per load. Tumble dry on low, then hang or drape them indoors for 24-48 hours to remove the last traces of moisture before storing them.

Make a cheap bivy bag for your sleeping bag by

using Tyvek Homewrap. Cut it about 6" larger than your sleeping bag measures when spread out flat. Fold it over your sleeping bag and secure it in place with binder clips from your office supplies. Cheap, compact, and waterproof!

Too hot to use your sleeping bag? Bring along a microfiber flat twin sheet. Instead of getting into your sleeping bag, lay on top of it for extra cushioning. Cover with the microfiber sheet to help keep insects at bay.

Sleeping bags are rated according to the temperatures that they should remain comfortable to sleep in at. Most summer bags are rated to 40 degrees F. To extend your comfort zone, use microfleece liners or add blankets to your bedroll.

In cold weather, always change your clothing before bed. Clothing worn during the daytime has picked up micro amounts of moisture from our skin and breath, and can mean chilly nights. Dry clothing reserved specifically for sleeping can keep you much warmer.

Kids' slumber bags are designed for indoor use, and

will not provide adequate warmth below 60 degrees F. For summer camping, they are usually adequate except at high altitudes. Adding a blanket can expand their comfort zone.

Air mattresses provide cushioning from the lumps and bumps of hard ground, but do not provide any insulation from cold air. Cover air mattresses with a comforter or blanket.

To keep beds clean in camp, roll them up in the morning. The rolled beds make great back rests for lounging in the tent during the day, if it turns out to be a rainy day. Cots can be stacked, if necessary, to give more floor space or rearranged to create seating. Air mattresses can be leaned against the tent wall, as they are lightweight and unlikely to puncture the tent fabric.

No sleeping bag? Bring blankets and comforters from home. Just remember to insulate yourself from the cold ground in cool weather. Blankets and comforters are much more bulky than sleeping bags, however.

Beverages

Put cold beverages in their own cooler to prevent frequent access to the cooler containing your food. This helps ice last longer with your food, as well as preventing cross contamination of beverage containers with fluids from raw food too.

Forgot the coffee pot? No problem! Make boiled coffee by adding coffee grounds to the water in a saucepan. Bring the mixture to a boil and boil for 3-5 minutes, depending on how strong you like your coffee. Remove from the heat and add a cup of cold water. The cold water will settle almost all of the grounds to the bottom of the pan, allowing you to carefully pour a precious cup of black gold into your cup.

Love your lattes? You can have them, espresso and all! Use any stovetop espresso pot on your camp stove, just like at home. Heat milk in a small saucepan and use a battery operated frother (get your milk in 1 c. shelf stable cartons), and you can have your gourmet treat in camp too. Best of all, an espresso pot is much more compact than a standard percolator is.

Got electricity? If you are camping with electricity available, your regular drip pot from home will work just fine. Some frequent campers buy an inexpensive drip pot just for traveling to keep their more expensive one in place at home.

Campfires

© G Miller 2014

Don't cut down trees for firewood—it burns poorly, and is usually against the law. It also will tend to produce more soot.

Roasting marshmallows—this campfire tradition used to be done on a stick, however, that has some issues today. First of all, some green sticks are obtained from poisonous plants or trees, hardly a great idea. Secondly, if everyone visiting a campground cut a sapling to make a marshmallow stick, none of them would be allowed to become new trees. Last of all, they require effort to find, then cut down. It's more ecologically sound to use a reusable metal roasting fork.

Keep roasting forks from stabbing by impaling the sharp points into old wine corks or a piece of Styrofoam from packing material.

To start a campfire—never ever use gasoline or white gas to start a fire! Start it like a pro with these simple (and much safer) fire starters: simply rub petroleum jelly into cotton balls until fully saturated. Place cotton balls in bag or container to carry along. To start the fire, surround 2-3 cotton balls with small sticks, twigs, and leaves. Light the cotton ball with a match, and surround your tiny fire with split firewood and larger sticks. You'll look like an old timer with this fast hack!

Another great fire starter is the logs sold in stores. Simply slice off a 1" thick slice and use that as a fire starter. It can be easily sliced with a serrated knife.

Don't bring firewood from home, even though it is tempting to do so to save money buying wood. Many insects and diseases are transmitted by transporting firewood from infected trees and bringing in wood is banned in many campgrounds for this reason. Don't be a "Typhoid Mary" with tree diseases or insect infestations!

Cooking on a campfire requires coals, not flames.

Let your fire burn down to just coals before trying to roast hotdogs, marshmallows, or to cook foil packets on the fire for best results.

No kindling? Use any corn or tortilla chip, such as Fritos or Doritos, as kindling for your campfire.

No firewood? Do like the pioneers did—collect dry cow chips. They burn well.

Want to amaze the kids? Start a fire with a magnifying glass on a sunny day. Or, write their initials on a piece of wood with the hot beam from that little magnifying lens. They'll be impressed for days!

Try baking on your campfire with a makeshift reflector oven. This version uses a large foil roasting pan, some aluminum foil, and a few sticks.

Place a doubled piece of heavy duty aluminum foil on top of the sticks as your pan. Put the items to be baked on the pan, after greasing it.

The aluminum foil pan is supported on the side of the fire by two sticks that have been pushed into the ground. Metal stakes, if long enough, could also be substituted. The foil pan will reflect the heat of the fire back and down onto the items being baked. For baking like this, you need a larger fire than would be used typically for cooking, especially since this simple design is not particularly efficient.

Campsites

Don't choose a campsite located in a depression or low area. If it rains, you are more likely to have problems with your tent or campsite flooding.

Don't dig a trench around your tent. Many older camping handbooks advocate this, but this actually does very little good and causes a great deal of harm to the natural environment you are hoping to enjoy.

Look up before pitching your tent. Don't set up camp with dead branches or dead trees overhead. There is a reason that these things are called widowmakers!

Don't camp alongside a creek or river, even if it is dry, especially in rainy weather. Rising water can flood your camp or even flash flood, washing you and your camp far down river.

In dry country, do not camp within 100 yards of a water source. Animals depend on the water source, both predator and prey. Your presence too close to the water disrupts the natural world.

When camping with a pet or hoping to enjoy relative peace, do not choose a campsite in close proximity to the restrooms, shower facilities, playground, on a corner or near the entrance. All of these things mean more traffic, both on foot and in vehicles.

Many campgrounds take reservations and many also fill up long before the weekend arrives. Make reservations and make sure you understand the cancellation policy. Most cancellations are going to cost you at least two nights of camping fees. Pay attention to minimum stay requirements at your chosen location as well.

Many campgrounds offer sites with electricity and water available at the campsite, and allow tents in the "RV" area where these amenities are available. Electricity means that you can use things such as electric heaters, fans, air conditioners (yes a tent can be cooled by an air conditioner!) hot plates, and coffee pots can be used, making your stay more comfortable. Fees are typically slightly higher than the "primitive" or "tent" area, but it may be worth the extra fee to have comfort amenities.

If possible, situate your tent on the west side of some large trees. That way, the sun is not immediately beating on your tent as it rises, allowing you the opportunity for a little extra shut eye before greeting the day.

Not all campsites are grassy. Bare ground campsites often become dust bowls. To keep the dust down, sprinkle the campsite with water during the day. Sprinkling used coffee grounds on the ground will also help keep the dust down, as well as keep ants away.

Cats

Cats are not always good travelers and may not enjoy camping. Like dogs, they must be kept on a leash or in a crate, and also need a litter box if kept in a crate.

Bring your cat's vaccination records along. Just like dogs, you may be required to show them to the park rangers.

Make sure your cat has a collar with an ID tag, in case of an escape.

Keep Kitty comfortable by offering plenty of fresh water, as well as shade.

Never leave your cat inside of a vehicle unattended. Temperatures rise rapidly and can cause death quickly.

Cell Phones

Cell phones allow us to stay connected to family, friends, and work. However, part of the appeal of camping is to escape those ties that bind. Restricting how accessible you are is a choice that should be made in advance of the camping trip.

Cell phones are very useful in the event of an emergency. These devices allow us to summon help quickly. However, they can also be distracting and consume all of one's time with instant messages, phone calls, and even games. Setting limits with children and teens about their use while camping is important so that everyone understands exactly what is expected before they even leave the house.

Many families restrict cell phone use to evenings or rainy days, with time limits set on how long the device may be used. If there are limited times to recharge the device, it may be easier for the user to fall in line with the family's expectations of when they can (and can't) use their device.

Due to thieves using social media outlets to find out when their victims are away from home, many families have concerns about posting information about their camping trip in real time. Communicate your concerns to your family and establish rules about what and when things can be shared.

For some families, privacy is a really big concern. If you don't want photos shared online by family members, establish the rule of "what happens in camp stays in camp" from the beginning and do not tolerate violations.

Checklist

Do like Santa Claus and make a list, then check it twice. It helps prevent things from being forgotten. Take along the list, and if something is not on the list but needed or wanted, it can go on the list for next time. If something turns out to not be needed or wanted, a note can be made to take it off of the list next time too.

Remember that season and location, as well as participants, will change your checklist. Cold weather and hot weather camping need many different things, just as different things are needed when kids are camping or it is all adults. Just like mountain camping with climbing as an activity would use different gear than a beach camp out with swimming and beach combing would use different items.

Cleaning

Forgot your scrubber?—Crumple a piece of aluminum foil, not too tightly (used foil works too!) and use that instead to scrub off persistent stuck-on food. Just don't use it on non-stick coated pans.

Coarse sand, along with soap and water, can also scour out stubborn stuck on grime in a pot.

Soot on your pots & pans: Rub the outside of the pots and pans, especially the bottom, with liquid dish washing liquid BEFORE using them on your camp stove or camp fire. Camp stoves are not as efficient at burning the fuel as your gas stove at home is, and often will leave a sooty residue as well. With the liquid soap coating, it washes off easily.

To clean out small dome tents—if you don't have a dust pan and small broom, simply remove the rain fly, pull out the stakes, and then pick up the tent, with the door facing downward. Shake the tent gently to loosen any debris and send it towards the door to fall to the ground.

Get sticky tree sap or rosin off of skin or hair by rubbing the area with mayonnaise. The sticky sap will seem to disappear!

Gum in hair? Rub peanut butter into the gum, gently separating the hair from the wad of gum. Wash hair after gum is removed.

Clothing

While car campers aren't facing the same issues as a backpacker, many of these hints can keep both happy.

Don't wear cotton clothing. It absorbs water as well as odors, and can become very smelly very quickly. Instead, choose wool or some of the new microfibers for rot resistance, quickly drying, and lightweight clothing.

Long sleeves and long pants help keep thorns and insects alike away from your skin. In dry climates, they can also slow evaporation of sweat from your skin as well, helping create a cool zone around your body.

In cold weather, wear a knit hat to help stay warm, even when sleeping.

Don't forget gloves, as they do more than merely keep your hands warm. Gloves can protect your hands from injuries from rocks, thorny brush, and even rope burns from working with ropes and cords. They don't have to be fancy or expensive—garden or work gloves or even the stretchy one-size-fits-all gloves will all work.

Gaiters work well to keep debris out of your shoes

and off of your socks, especially when hiking in shorts.

Don't forget the rain gear. Rain doesn't mean your camping trip is a disaster, so be prepared to cope with rain by having rain ponchos or rain suits for everyone. Being comfortable and continuing to enjoy activities despite the rain will salvage the trip.

In cool weather, dress in layers for maximum comfort. Layers can be added or removed to maintain comfortable body temperatures no matter what the activity level.

See this woman? She's wearing a tank top, topped with a t-shirt, then a hoodie, and finally an insulated flannel shirt. She also had a pair of jogging pants on over capris, and was wearing gloves. All she had to add at this point was a knit hat! None of her clothing was high tech or special outdoor clothing, and most of it had seen years of use. Granted, she was car camping, not backpacking, where every ounce of weight counts.

Have a pair of camp shoes, which are lightweight, comfortable shoes to wear in camp instead of your hiking shoes or boots. It's kind of like having slippers on steroids—they are quick to slip on for midnight runs to the bathroom and comfortable for wearing around camp.

For both sun and bug protection, buy several lightweight men's dress shirts with long sleeves from a thrift store. If they are stained or destroyed, you are only out a few dollars, and they offer great sun protection. They also make great swimsuit cover-ups.

Don't forget the jackets! At high altitude, temperatures often drop at night and it can be chilly even in midsummer. Having jackets will make camping more fun.

Wear a hat. Hats offer more than decoration, they help shield your head and face from sun and its burning rays, as well as increasing your warmth when temperatures plummet.

Don't be a fashion plate in the campground. Skip the fashion concerns. Outdoor clothing is all about functionality. Look for sturdy designs with pockets, made from wicking and quick drying fabrics. Many companies offer pants that zip down to make shorts, and long sleeved shirts that the sleeves roll up or zip off entirely.

Bring pajamas. In summer, this can be shorts and a tank top. In winter, bring something warmer. Many people opt for sweats or microfiber long underwear for winter pajamas. Remember that in a campground, any midnight bathroom excursions will be done in those pajamas so make practicality a goal.

Pack clothes compactly using "space bags" that vacuum out excess air. A low cost alternative is to pack individual outfits into gallon sized plastic bags, pressing out the air and sealing the resealable strip.

If you are hiking or doing lots of walking, make sure to have plenty of clean socks. Two pairs per day is average, although they can be washed out and dried by clipping to the outside of your backpack during the day with binder clips. Clean socks keep your feet drier and less likely to blister.

Cooking and Food

Special food is not necessary when camping. You don't *have* to eat freeze dried meals or dine out of cans, nor even survive on grilled foods. Any recipe you use at home can be adapted to use when camping, although trying to make an angel food cake from scratch is probably not a good idea. There are numerous cookbooks with ideas and recipes, but any stovetop recipe is going to be fairly easy to duplicate while camping.

Arriving at your campsite late on Friday night? Speed up dinner by pre-cooking it at home or buying it from the deli. Fried or rotisserie chicken, along with salad, can be a delicious start to the weekend. Use paper plates for easy clean up before bed too. Sandwiches can also be easy, served on just a paper towel.

Prevent contamination—seal raw meats tightly and then place into a second container to prevent any fluids from contaminating the other food items or the ice that is being used to keep the food cold. Fluids from raw meats can contain bacteria that can make people very sick and prevention is far better than treatment. Besides, do you really want people to remember the camp trip for who ended up in the hospital with food poisoning?

Prep raw meat at home—Do your prepping of raw meat, whether it is shaping patties or cutting it up, at home where you have access to hot water and soap to decontaminate your hands and utensils. In camp, avoid touching the raw meat directly, using tongs or a spatula to handle the meat. Don't forget to wash utensils thoroughly.

Add marinades and seasonings to meat at home—for weekend trips, add your seasonings or marinades at home for maximum flavor and minimal fuss in camp.

Use the K.I.S.S. theory—that stands for Keep It Simple, Stupid. Don't fuss over meals when camping. Plan for simple foods that are easily prepared and opt for the gourmet dining when you have time at home.

Appetites are bigger when camping—plan on

healthy snacks and prepare them at home so that they are easy to grab and eat, whether it is raw vegetables, fruit, or something else.

Easy to use butter—try the soft margarine in the squeeze bottle or the spray on versions for easy use in camp, whether it is for morning pancakes or a roasted ear of corn. The bottles are much easier to manage in the cooler and take up less space as well.

Cooking oil—trying to keep things minimalist? Reuse one of the water bottle flavoring containers, such as Mio or one of the other brands. Just pop off the top, rinse it thoroughly, and let it air dry overnight before filling with cooking oil for your backpack. It gives very accurate dispensing and doesn't leak.

Pie Irons—these are fun to use, and make meal preparation easy too. Best advice, have one for each child to prevent squabbles over who's turn it is now. Everything from grilled cheese to pocket pizzas can be made in these handy little gadgets. By buttering the bread and using canned pie filling for the centers, it can also create a tasty little fruit pie too! Wrapping the pie iron in aluminum foil makes clean up a breeze too.

Make popcorn in camp with Jiffy Pop. The expanding container amuses the kids as well as the more grown up kids, and it's a tasty snack too.

Bring along a stovetop percolator even if you don't drink coffee. Without the stem and basket, the coffeepot makes an excellent and efficient way to heat water for everything from instant soups to hot water for washing up.

Check out recipes for freezer bag and foil pouch cooking. It allows customized meals that are easy to prepare.

Like drip coffee? Compact on-the-mug versions are available, including silicone models that collapse. Just add a filter, coffee grounds and boiling water to drip coffee straight into your mug. Just as good as at home!

Do it like the pioneers who crossed the country in covered wagons! Get a cast iron dutch oven and bake in your campfire. It takes a bit of practice, but delicious results will occur. For baking in the campfire, buy the type with a rimmed flat lid to hold the coals.

Roast dinner in the campfire. Potatoes are a natural to wrap in foil and bake in the campfire. Meat, besides hot dogs, can be roasted on cooking forks too. Try skewering chunks of steak, sprinkling with seasonings, and cooking to taste on the fire.

Want chips in camp? Use single serving size to prevent overindulging or chips getting stale and soggy.

Coolers

Freeze water in gallon jugs for using in your cooler for a low cost solution to chilling food. As the ice melts, the water will stay inside the jug, keeping the cooler dryer inside.

Use a separate cooler for beverages to keep the food cooler cold longer.

Not all coolers are created equally. Look for coolers that are rated for 5 or 7 days for best results.

Keep the coolers in the shade for maximum cooling and to keep ice longer.

In hot, dry climates, drape a damp towel over the cooler top to help keep it cooler longer. Reapply as necessary through the day.

Freeze water bottles that have been refilled, leaving 1" headspace in each bottle for the expansion of the ice. They'll keep your food cold without getting it wet when it melts. The smaller sized bottles work great for smaller coolers.

Frozen food stays cold longer, as much as 2 days

longer. Freeze meats that are to be cooked later in the trip for week long trips and they will be thawed and ready to cook in 3-4 days.

Destinations

Don't camp at the same place all the time.
Familiarity might make things easier, but new places offer new activities and new experiences too. After all, variety IS the spice of life!

Research potential destinations online ahead of time. Find out what the location offers for activities and what amenities are available in the campground.

Attend special events occasionally. Most campers may want to avoid crowds usually, but sometimes, a special event offers a brand new experience that you cannot miss. Try a festival once in a while.

Got kids? I bet they have opinions and interests too. Ask them what they would like to do or see, and you might get a surprise or two. Trying the things that interest them may provide a great bonding experience as well. It will also make them feel as though their interests and wishes are also important enough to matter.

Try a variety of camping styles, both primitive and

with amenities such as electricity, for a varied experience. Getting out of your comfort zone helps maintain flexibility and adaptability too.

Keep a list of parks you have visited and the campsite you stayed at, along with a rating of the experience. Try out county, state, national parks, and national forests to see which you prefer.

Review parks and campgrounds online to help other campers find the best of the best. List what you do like as well as what you did not like about the park in your review.

Start a bucket list of destinations. Which parks are you hoping to visit, even if they are distant from where you live? What appeals to you about those parks?

Dishes

Just like at home, nobody wants to do dishes. Encourage self-sufficiency by having everyone wash their own plate or bowl and utensils. Marking names with water resistant tape will help prevent anyone claiming they'd already washed their dishes when they hadn't.

For camping, use unbreakable dishes out of plastic, melamine or enameled metal. Collapsible ones made from silicone are also available. Get different colors for each person if you can to help keep it straight.

Meals cooked in the campfire in foil packets keep dishes to a minimum, as does freezer bag cooking. Try these methods to vary the routine.

A metal mixing bowl makes a great "sink" for washing dishes, and does double duty for other kitchen tasks as well.

Use flexible cutting mats as your cutting board. They take up little space, weigh very little, and wash easily.

Instead of bringing steak or paring knives, assign everyone a pocket knife to use. They work for everything from cutting sandwiches to cutting up vegetables for dinner. In addition, they are compact to pack and can be carried in a pocket.

Instead of buying new eating utensils for camping, hit thrift stores and garage sales. It's recycling at its best and will save you money.

Dogs

Dogs are man's best friend, and a common camping companion. These hacks help your buddy stay on everyone's good side, from the park ranger to the squirrels.

Barking—Almost all dogs bark some, but the key in a campground is to not annoy everyone within hearing distance or keep them awake at night. If your dog is prone to barking at everything, blocking their vision of other campers and activities may help keep the barking to a minimum. Some people may choose to use a crate that has had three sides covered to give the dog a view to the front only (wire crates have better ventilation for summer use.) Others may opt to keep the pet inside the tent much of the time. If your dog absolutely will not stop barking, especially at night, it may be best to board them with a kennel, veterinarian, or a friend while you are camping.

Campsite—Almost all campgrounds require someone to be with the pet at all times in the campground. While

I have never had a problem with leaving them alone while using the showers or toilet, that should be kept to a minimum as well. In addition, pets are usually not allowed inside of any park building. Follow the rules and if you are uncertain, ask the rangers.

Crates—Crates can make a dog feel that they have a safe haven, especially if they use a crate at home. Wire crates offer better ventilation, helping keep them cooler. To increase the cooling power, draping the crate with wet towels (squeeze out excess water so they don't drip) to allow the natural evaporation process to help cool the crate. Make sure your pet is in the shade to prevent heat stroke. Keep their water dish or bottle full as well, to help them to stay hydrated. In very hot weather, some dogs may need more help to stay comfortable, using a fan blowing over a pan of ice, cold packs in their crate, or even air conditioning. Short faced dogs such as bulldogs, pugs, boxers, etc., are often prone to distress quickly in hot weather, as are older dogs, heavy coated dogs, and dogs that are recovering from an illness.

Crates are also a great way to safely secure your pet

at night in the tent while you are sleeping.

Dishes—if you are being weight and space conscious, you may wish to consider the collapsible dishes made from coated canvas for your pet. They fold up, hold water or food reliably, and weigh very little.

Dishes—While many people bring along the same dishes that they use for Fido or Fluffy at home, others prefer something less expensive to take along in case of loss or damage. It's a great way to reuse the plastic containers that things such as margarine, sour cream, yogurt, or frozen whipped topping come in.

Food—Bringing along the big bag of kibble may be fine if you are feeding a giant dog on a two week camp out, but most of us have smaller dogs and shorter stays while camping. Prepackage their food into recycled containers or a plastic bag for easy single meal dispensing. This also makes it easy if you have multiple dogs along that eat different food. The prepackaged food can then be put into a larger container—my favorite is an ice cream bucket, which has a handle as well as a lid.

Food—Most people use kibble, of one brand or another, to feed their dog. While your dog may be picky, as well as messy about his or her eating habits, this can lead to unwanted visitors, often of the black and white type. Skunks and raccoons are both highly attracted to spilled or discarded dog food, and will come calling to dine if you leave it where they can find it. That means picking up every single tidbit that Fido or Fluffy spills! It may be advisable to feed a smaller portion that has been "doctored" with something yummy, which can be chicken broth from a can, canned food, bacon grease, or some of your own dinner leftovers, to get your pet to eat all of their food relatively quickly. Don't leave the dish out for snacking or the local raccoons or skunks are apt to come to dinner too.

ID Tags—Nobody likes to lose their pet, but every year, hundreds if not thousands, of pets disappear during camping trips and vacations, often in an entirely different state than the one they live in. Make sure that your dog has an ID tag attached to their collar with a phone number that is good while you are on vacation or your camping trip, not your home or office number for when you are at home.

Leashes—Dogs are typically required to remain on leash at all time in almost all campgrounds, state parks, national parks, etc. They also often restrict the length of the leash to 6' or 10'. Know the rules and abide by them, as frequent violations from pet owners leads to banning dogs from parks.

The boxer on the previous page has a reflective leash, highly visible even in the pitch dark as it reflects even small amounts of light. The round shape is also more difficult for persistent leash biters to chew through. For the truly devout leash biters, a chain or coated cable lead may be necessary.

This dog, a devout destroyer of leashes, is fastened to a short cable (like is used to secure trailers and bicycles) that then slides along a longer cable that is run between trees at ground level. A carbiner provides the slide with minimal friction. She also happens to be a very old dog, so she is not as active as she once was. This arrangement keeps her safely restrained, while allowing her to move in and out of the shade as she likes.

Muzzle—Just because a dog wears a muzzle does not mean it is "mean"! It means that they may be a bit nervous around strangers, and their owners are making sure a bite or nip does not happen. For those who have nervous dogs, remember that children are not leashed and can appear out of seemingly nowhere to grab your dog, and your dog will think it is under attack and respond accordingly. The muzzle is to protect your dog, not the stranger or child, from accusations of biting. Most muzzles will allow your dog to drink while muzzled, something that can be important on a hot summer day.

People Food—Some people never give their dogs "people food", while others do occasionally. Some feed it daily. Whichever category you fall in, the time to change categories may not be on your camping trip. Sudden changes in diet can result in diarrhea and vomiting, which is never appreciated on your sleeping bag at 3 a.m. while it is raining. Nearly equal in noxious factor is an attack of gas resulting from suddenly receiving meat scraps that the dog is not accustomed to eating. "Green clouds from the bog of eternal stench" may dissipate quickly outdoors, but your tent is technically indoors, and it won't vanish that quickly! Keep treats from your steak to a minimum and everyone will win in the long run.

Treats—we all tend to indulge in more snack foods and treats when we are camping than we do at home. It's part of the whole escaping from the normal routine and reality of our daily lives, it seems. Your pet will want treats too. While you may opt to give them more liberally than you do at home, it is best to stick to the same type that is used at home. Many dogs are happy receiving pieces of kibble as a treat through the day.

Vaccination Records—some parks and campgrounds require you to physically bring a vaccination record with you to show that your pet is fully vaccinated. Keeping a copy of your pet's records in your car is a very good idea.

Waste—Okay, nobody LIKES doing it, but it still has to be done. Pick up the waste from your dog doing his or her *"thing"*, whether it is in the campground or on the trail. For big dogs, it's a great way to re-use grocery bags. There are also handy dispensers that can attach to your leash and hold disposal bags for collecting waste. This keeps it off of everyone's shoes as well as helps control the spread of diseases and parasites. Besides, who wants to see a bunch of ancient dog doo littering the area?

Water—some pets have touchy stomachs. If your dog has an easily upset one, bringing water from home for them to drink while on your camping trip may prevent bouts of vomiting or diarrhea.

Water—don't forget to make sure Fido or Fluffy have a ready supply of fresh, clean water while camping. Check their water or offer them water every time you get thirsty to make sure your buddy stays hydrated.

Never leave your dog inside of a vehicle unattended. Temperatures rapidly soar inside of a vehicle and can result in death very soon.

Do not let your dog chase wildlife. It's often illegal, and it is not a good habit to encourage, as pets can quickly chase an animal far enough away that they become disoriented and lost.

Remember, your dog lives in a house with you, and when in the great outdoors, may need a coat just as much as you do. These can be purchased at most stores selling pet supplies or easily made at home by the average home sewer.

This boxer has very short, thin hair and chills easily even in moderately cold temperatures. She is wearing a fleece coat on this early spring camping trip.

Duffle Bags

Duffle bags come in a variety of prices, sizes, and materials. This flexible nature means that they are a natural for camping.

Hate fighting your tent to get it small enough for the bag that it came with? Save hassles, and buy a larger duffle bag of the same or slightly longer length. Your tent will pack easier and you will spend less time muttering curses under your breath too. Buy one large enough to hold stakes, mallet, ground cloth, spare tarp, spare cord, and the tent and you'll have an all-in-one package.

Use duffle bags to keep camp gear organized. A giant sized duffle bag can keep all of the sleeping bags together at home, then carry them on the camping trip.

Give each family member a different color duffle bag to pack their clothes in for the trip. The different colors make it easier to locate the right bag for the right person.

For families with multiple tents used for different

purposes, use a small duffle bag to carry cord, mallet, extra tarp, tent stakes, whisk broom, dustpan, and other items used with more than one tent. This way, extra sets are not required with each tent, nor is there a frantic hunt to figure out where the supplies are located at.

Use a duffle bag to keep beach supplies organized. Typical items to include would be beach toys, Frisbee, towels, swimsuits, beach blanket, sunscreen, and umbrella for shade.

Use a small duffle bag to keep travel materials ad mementos together while traveling. This will prevent them from being damaged or lost, as well as keep them neatly confined.

First Aid

All campers should carry a first aid kit along in their vehicle or backpack.

Your first aid and medication kit should include any prescribed medications as well as OTC medications that are used regularly.

Include typical wound care items such as bandages, gauze, tape, hydrogen peroxide, anti-bacterial cream, etc. that your family typically prefers.

Include tweezers for removing stickers and splinters in your first aid kit.

Fishing

Fishing is a common pastime when camping. While it can require fancy and expensive gear, fishing at its simplest requires little more than a cane pole, some string, and a hook. Most people fish somewhere in between.

Dispose of fishing line properly. Don't leave it laying at water's edge to tangle wildlife. It can kill wildlife.

Fish legally. Buy a license and observe all regulations for the water you are fishing in.

Practice leave no trace when fishing too. Pack out your trash, whether it is bait containers or dead fish.

Flashlights and Lanterns

Kids love flashlights, but parents hate buying batteries. Go kid powered by buying the kids "shake" lights that have a charger inside that charges the flashlight by shaking the entire flashlight. Self-charging flashlights are also available in crank models.

Save money by choosing lights that use the same battery size—Lanterns and flashlights are both available that use AA batteries, which are also readily available in rechargeable. By using the same size battery in all of your lights, it's easier to have spares.

Get micro lanterns for use in your tent—these pocket size lanterns are light enough to hang from the center of most tents, providing adequate illumination for most tasks. Larger lanterns are too heavy to hang and must be supported by some other means or set on the floor where they do not illuminate as well. Having a light hanging in your tent means it is much easier to find it in the dark, should a middle of the night event occur.

Headlamps are great for accomplishing tasks in the

dark when two hands are needed, such as setting up your tent. Some have their own headband, while others attach to a ball cap.

Need a nightlight? Use glow sticks for safe nightlights inside a tent.

Kerosene lanterns, while they look rustic and romantic, are not efficient in terms of lighting. They give off a yellow light that does not illuminate brightly.

Propane and white gas lanterns both use mantles, which have to be installed properly for best results. Make sure you have the right type mantle for your lantern, as they vary between models. Always carry a spare or two as well.

Take extra fuel for your lantern whenever possible. Sometimes propane tanks seem to not last as long as others. Tipping over a white gas lantern can result in a fuel spill, requiring the lantern to be refilled.

No lantern, no problem! Strap a head lamp to a full jug of water to create a less direct, more ambient light suitable for at the table or in the tent.

Like a bit of light around the campsite to help

prevent tripping and falls? Pick up a dozen or two of the inexpensive stake style solar lights and stick them around your campsite. The sunlight will charge them and you'll see where that root sticks up out of the ground easier.

Furniture

Bring along camp chairs or stools. Having a comfortable seat can make camping much more enjoyable. Don't forget the kids—they enjoy comfort too!

Hate sleeping on the ground, even with a sleeping pad? You don't have to! Cots are available in a variety of sizes, and typically are either military style with stretcher bars that are placed in the ends or scissor style that unfold just like camp chairs do. Other models simply fold in half. The easiest to use are the scissoring models, which are also very compact for transporting. They aren't light, however, and you will not want to pack them far from your car. They also take up more room. Calculate at least 2 "people" per adult cot in tent ratings. Example-Tent A is rated for 6 people. It will probably hold 2 cots and might hold 3. Tent B is rated for 12 people, and will probably hold 4-5 adult cots, and might hold 6. In addition, tent measurements are taken at the floor, not 24" up. With sloping walls, the actual available space is much smaller than the floor measurement is. Another alternative is air mattresses, which come in both single height (the height of a mattress alone) and raised configurations. Raised air beds typically achieve roughly the same height as a platform bed. Some models combine cot and air mattress for as large as queen size bed!

When primitive camping, sites often do not include a picnic table. While it is possible to camp without a table, those with aching backs or stiff knees may appreciate the ability to cook, eat, and prepare meals at a higher level than the ground. There are a variety of tables available, ranging from the type that simply has fold up legs to those that collapse completely to take up no more space than a folding camp chair. Table tops also include a variety of surfaces, including fabric, wood, metal, and plastic. Choose the model that works best for you.

Want more kitchen convenience? Folding kitchen set ups are available from companies such as Coleman to make camp cooking. Some even include a kitchen sink!

Use a sturdy, weather proof container to hold camping gear for easy transport and storage. Strong containers do double duty as a seat in camp. Find suitable containers at home improvement stores, looking for ratings that hold over 300 lbs. These containers cost more than the lightweight ones sold in dollar stores and discount chains, but they will last for years, even while being sat on. They also make great "night stands" in the tent.

Fold up chairs and place them under a canopy or tarp at night to keep them dry. You may want to use them in the tent if you have a rainy day, and it's much easier if they aren't already wet.

When walking through campgrounds, pay attention to the type of furniture that other campers are using. You may get new ideas from these observations. Asking the campers about their equipment is often a great ice breaker, and you may find out about a great idea too.

Gear

Bungee cords are useful "extras" to have along on a camping trip. With their handy hooks and elastic strap, they can do many things from securing a sleeping pad in a roll to fastening a tarp down in gusty wind.

Tarps are very useful and serve many purposes from providing shade to sheltering from rain or wind. Wrapped around open doors on your car, they can also create a tiny changing room.

Clothespins can do more than merely hang wet swimsuits up to dry. They can clip a bag of chips closed, weight down a room divider in a tent, anda hundred other things.

Spare batteries are an essential. Don't leave home without them.

Glamping

Glamping is a new term and is a combination of glamor and camping. It refers to a more luxurious experience than the typical tent-and-sleeping-bag experience will deliver.

DIY glamping is possible, rather than paying astronomical fees to stay at a glamping resort. Think luxury as you choose your setup.

DIY glamping will likely require a much larger vehicle or cargo trailer to haul all of the accessories required. A campsite that has electricity and allows large tents is also almost a must-have.

Grills and grilling

Camping almost requires at least the occasional grilled meal. Know your options before leaving home.

Folding portable grills are available to use over an open fire. For grilling over wood, this type of grill is almost essential. Always let your wood fire die down to a bed of coals before grilling food or you will have more charring than grilling going on.

Portable propane grills that use the 1 lb. disposable cylinders are available. Most are designed for table top use, and are suitable for burgers, chops, hotdogs, small steaks, and other simple foods. Don't try to slow cook a brisket over one of these grills, as it is too small and lack precise heat control like is found on larger units.

Disposable charcoal grills are another option without making a large investment. Essentially these are a large foil pan with charcoal inside and topped with a thin metal grill. These grills are best suited to foods that cook quickly, as the charcoal cannot be replenished inside for longer cooking.

Portable charcoal grills are available, and typically are capable of cooking more food at one time, as well as accomplishing more complex grilling tasks. Charcoal can be added for longer cooking as well. Look for models with a domed lid to keep the heat in for slower grilling foods or cooking in colder weather. Some models also come with a case for transporting the grill in, minimizing mess in your vehicle from camping or tailgating.

Larger portable grills will use the larger tanks of propane, and offer more space as well as their own collapsible stands. These are very popular with tailgaters, making them readily available for campers as well.

Why use a portable grill with charcoal or propane while camping? It's simple—convenience. Stooping and bending over a campfire grill is not everyone's idea of a great activity and may be actually painful or impossible for some.

Hammocks

Here, I am sleeping with a large dog in a rope hammock with spreader bars. Most large dogs are not enthusiastic about sleeping in a hammock, but this dog is very spoiled and not afraid of many things. It was also the first time she had tried a hammock out.

Not all campgrounds allow hammocks to be hung from trees. If not, to use a hammock, you must have a hammock stand to hold it.

Camping hammocks are made from thin nylon fabric and are often referred to as "parachute silk" although it is not actually silk. These hammocks are cooler in summer than cotton hammocks and dry almost instantly. They hang from a rope loop on either end of the hammock.

Entire books have been written about hammock camping, and advocates swear by it instead of using a tent.

Hammocks encourage one to relax on a hot summer afternoon to read or listen to music.

For those interested in ultra-light backpacking, hammocks are very popular and worth considering. Watch the numerous videos available on YouTube for more detailed information about hammocks.

Hiking

Stay on trails. This protects the plants and animals that live alongside it.

Use a hiking stick (also known as a staff). It improves balance, and can help probe to see how deep a stream is, whether ground is firm, move vegetation out of the way, etc. too. They can also become tent poles or tarp supports.

Practice leave no trace. Pack out your own trash and any trash you find, as a good neighbor in the hiking community.

Wear bear bells in bear country, and carry bear spray as a precaution. Bear spray is a high powered version of pepper spray, as normal pepper spray seems more like a seasoning than a deterrent to a bear. Never approach a bear, even a baby bear. (Mama will be nearby.) Always retreat cautiously when spotting a bear ahead.

Carry water and basic first aid/survival gear along even on day hikes. Include a signaling whistle.

Don't count on your cell phone or GPS device to work when hiking. They may fail due to batteries or lack of a good signal. Carry a paper map as back up.

Laundry

For the average weekend camper, laundry in the campground is not an issue. However, they often do have facilities for doing laundry, which can be useful in the event of a disaster. For the just-in-case laundry, bring along a sample size laundry detergent or put a small amount of soap into a smaller container for transporting.

Wet towels and swim suits after swimming or showers can be hung on a line stretched between trees, if allowed in the park. If the lines between trees are not allowed, lay them on the hood of your car/truck/van. They'll still dry quickly in the summer sun. In not-so-warm weather, put them on the dash of your car.

Insects

Instant grits keep ants out of your campsite. Just sprinkle them around, and the ants will stay at bay.

Fire ants hate coffee. Sprinkle your used coffee grounds around any of them that opt to invade your space and they will vacate. Liberally sprinkle them around a campsite to ensure that they don't come calling while you are camping.

Hydrocortisone cream, available at any drugstore, will help stop the itching and heal insect bites or stings. Just rub it into the affected area 3-4 times daily.

Don't forget the insect repellant! Mosquitoes and other biting insects can turn a camping trip into an exercise in agony quickly without it.

Do an evening tick check on everyone to help keep ticks at bay and prevent Lyme disease. Tick removal requires that the tick be forced to withdraw its head from the skin before removal or infection can result. Many methods are advocated for doing so, including dabbing with liquid soap, touching with a hot match head, putting on a drop of alcohol, etc. Saving the tick if it has been attached for very long is also advised so that the insect can be tested for Lyme disease. Pay particular attention to the head, where hair may prevent easy observation of a tick's presence.

To help reduce tick infestations, spray clothing and shoes with insect repellent containing DEET. Pay particular attention to collars, the cuffs of sleeves, tops of shoes, and tops of socks, as well as waist bands.

Check pets each evening for the presence of ticks and remove them as necessary.

Not all tents have no-see-um proof mesh on windows and vents. To help reduce their numbers, spray the mesh itself with insect repellant containing DEET.

To reduce the number of lurking mosquitoes in your campsite, burn a citronella candle, lamp or torch during the evening.

Sensitive individuals can avoid DEET and other ingredients found in insect repellants by using alternatives such as Avon's Skin So Soft or Johnson's creamy baby oil.

Burning sage in your campfire can reduce the number of lurking mosquitoes in camp.

If stung by a bee, do not pull the stinger out as this will force more venom into the sting site. Instead, scrape the stinger away with a knife or credit card.

Baking soda, combined with water to make a paste, will help take the pain away from stings and painful insect bites.

Scrapbook Page

Make a scrapbook page at home for each camping trip, capturing memories while they are still fresh. Getting participation from the entire family makes it even more fun. Include photos, small treasures such as leaves, brief descriptions written by each member of the family, etc. on the page.

Encourage each child to write a brief piece about the camping trip, focusing on something such as their favorite part, the scariest part, the silliest part, etc. Writing about the trip is educational and good practice for the child as well as a way to preserve memories.

Don't let teens off the hook for writing a brief piece about the camping trip. All too soon, they will be leaving home. Preserving their last years at home is an opportunity you don't want to miss. They will also treasure the pages later in life, even if they may think it is "silly" now.

Stoves

There a number of different types of stoves available for use by the camper. Choosing the right one for you is important, as it is how you are going to prepare your food while camping.

Alcohol stoves—these can be homemade from an aluminum can and burn denatured alcohol. These are reliable but offer only basic heating ability suitable for boiling water. These are lightweight and easy to use, and remain popular with minimalist backpackers. Their best use is heating water to rehydrate meals and make hot drinks.

Esbit stoves—these stoves use a chemical tablet that burns very hot and very quickly. They are a great emergency stove, but offer only a very hot flame that is suitable for quickly heating water to boiling. They are also reliable stoves. Their best use is rehydrating meals and making hot drinks. Their con is that the tablets can be hard to find locally and expensive to purchase.

Liquid fuel ("Coleman gas") stoves—these stoves

come in both single burner and double burner models. The fuel is pressurized by pumping a hand pump. After priming and lighting, the fuel is heated by the flame for greater efficiency. These stoves are classics and have been in use a very long time. The larger versions are not suited to backpacking, as they are heavy and bulky. Smaller, more compact and lighter versions are available as well. These have a compact burner that often has folding legs, and the tank is attached by a small diameter hose. These smaller tanks also have a hand pump for pressurizing. Most of these stoves are also reliable classics. Most will also simmer as well as quickly bring water to a boil, making them more versatile for cooking more complex meals.

Propane stoves—are available in single, double, and triple models, as well as larger burners designed for large boiling or frying pots. These are very nearly identical to cooking on your stove at home in their operation. Smaller models also are designed to use disposable 1 lb. gas canisters, making them easier to pack along. Propane stoves are generally not a good choice for backpacking, but are a great choice for car camping and tailgating.

Pocket stoves are designed to burn almost anything small and are compact for packing. They burn paper, small twigs, small pinecones, grass knots, cow chips, or about anything that is small enough to fit into the fire chamber and is combustible. Because of their small fire chamber, they are not good for simmering for long periods or cooking anything that requires steady medium hot to hot heat levels. They are best suited to reheating canned or cooked foods or boiling water for rehydrating food or making hot drinks. They also make good backup stoves or emergency stoves. They are also low cost, which makes them very attractive for emergency preparation.

Sterno stoves—are designed to burn Sterno, a type of gelled alcohol. They are not particularly hot and do not boil water quickly. However, they can be used to simmer food for slow cooking. Many people use this type of stove as their emergency or back up stove. Sterno is also used to keep food hot at outdoor events and buffets.

Kerosene stoves are no longer commonly seen in the USA, although they do remain popular in other countries. Where kerosene is readily available, they can be a reliable alternative. Kerosene stoves typically use a wick to supply the fuel.

Butane stoves are also available. Butane is sold for these stoves either in the squat cans or in a hairspray type can, depending on the type of stove used. While they remain popular with backpackers, the small butane canisters must be packed in and then packed out as empties afterwards. Some backpackers object to this and are prompted to choose alternative stoves. The hairspray like canisters are used in a larger square stove and these stoves are also popular with caterers, which attests to their versatility and reliability. These stoves are easy to use while car camping.

When stove shopping, read descriptions and reviews alike to determine which stove is most likely to suit your needs. Many people own more than one type of stove (I own about six different ones.) Different stoves work best in different circumstances. Most novice campers find either the propane or the butane stoves to be the least complicated and intimidating.

Read your owner's manual and understand how to operate and troubleshoot your stove before taking it camping. Practice using it at home to cook in your own kitchen to ensure confidence in camp.

Sunburn

Aloe vera juice will take the sting out of a sunburn. Just buy a bottle, like is sold for drinking, at any health food store. Keep it in your cooler and apply liberally to any sunburned area for instant relief.

Prevent sunburn by applying sunscreen each morning and re-applying as necessary through the day.

Tents

Tents are your home away from home and your personal castle in the campground. They come in many sizes, prices, shapes, and materials too. They provide a shaded, insect resistant, and hopefully waterproof refuge at the end of the day.

Ground cloth—Don't skip it. It keeps moisture from migrating through your tent floor, as well as keeping your tent floor cleaner. That all helps your tent to last longer, as well as keeping you dryer. While expensive foot prints are available for middle to upper tier priced tents, they are not essential. A lightweight tarp (or multiple tarps for large tents) will work quite well. Just remember to tuck any excess tarp protruding out from under your tent back under itself until it is no longer protruding from the edge of the tent. If you don't, you will actually cause water to run under the tent floor, increasing the amount that will migrate through your floor and end up dampening bedrolls and anything else in contact with the floor.

Keep the weight down when backpacking by using Tyvek Homewrap for a footprint under your tent. It's lightweight and waterproof.

Holes—buy a package of adhesive ripstop nylon patches and keep them with your tent. Holes can appear for a variety of reasons, ranging from something rubbing on the tent while in storage to a flying camp fire ember, and are best patched immediately, when possible. The adhesive patches may not exactly match your tent, but they will restore its usefulness as your shelter. Follow the directions on the package, but most are simply a case of peel off the backing and adhere to the tent fabric.

Seam Sealing—buy a container of seam sealer every spring and make it a habit to seal the seams of both the rain fly and the tent itself before the first camping trip of the year. Always seal the seams of a new tent to prevent leaks on its debut voyage into the great outdoors.

Spare tarp—many a camping trip has been salvaged by the ready access of a spare tarp. The spare tarp can become a rain fly when your old standby suddenly starts resembling a sieve by simply putting it over the tent, and using paracord and stakes to secure it on top of the tent. It can also become a quick windbreak, provide shade on a hot summer day, or provide shelter for cooking outdoors when a rain shower decides to arrive.

Tent Stakes—tent stakes are not all created equal, and almost all new tents arrive with crappy tent stakes. Buy better ones, and remember that different ground conditions mean different stakes are necessary. Very loose, sandy ground means long V or Y shaped stakes to grip securely, while rocky, hard ground fares better with the wire-like metal stakes. Extra tent stakes are handy too, in case one bends or breaks. Don't forget the stakes for securing your rain fly properly either.

Heating—tents can be heated safely with electric heaters when electricity is available. Small forced air units with fans or oil filled radiators are both good choices. Place the small forced air units on a raised surface to ensure that sleeping bags and other bedding do not come in contact with the heater (crates work great and are also great for carrying smaller objects along) and keep them away from tent walls and other flammable surfaces. Propane fueled "buddy" heaters are also available, but are riskier to use in a tent due to the presence of actual flame.

Fans—Summertime heat can turn a tent into a sauna during midday, making napping difficult or impossible inside. Often, temperatures remain high even after sundown. Opening windows helps increase air flow to cool the tent, and a fan may also be necessary. Numerous models of battery operated fans, often with integrated lights, are available. When electricity is available, any fan from home can also be used.

Can't take the heat? You don't have to switch to a travel trailer or motorhome! Some tent models have a built in port for a window air conditioner, and others can be modified to have a port for the air conditioner. Small units, typically 5000 or 8000 BTU units, are best suited to cooling a tent. Some people increase the efficiency of the air conditioner by laying a space blanket on top of the tent and under the rainfly to help keep the cool in and the hot sun out. The air conditioners typically rest on a raised surface (often a milk crate) to keep them above the ground and low in the tent. Be smart and only run the unit when you are using the tent.

Electricity—if electricity is available at your campsite, you'll want to bring along the things you need to enjoy it. This will typically include a heavy duty extension cord rated for outdoor use and a plug in strip to allow multiple things to be plugged in. Bring the cord in through the e-port on your tent or the door if your tent lacks an e-port.

Replace your guy lines for your tent and rainfly with reflective cord to prevent tripping over the cord at night. Reflective cord is available from many outdoor gear suppliers.

Want a little bit of luxury in your tent that helps keep the cold at bay? Bring along the interlocking rubber foam play mat pieces, which measure 24" square, to cover the tent floor. Great insulation & cushy surface that packs up into a stack of squares.

Hate muddy paths leading to your tent? Beat the

mud and rain with a portable walkway. Buy 1x2" furring strips, cutting the 8' long boards into 24" lengths. Next, using a staple gun, staple poly straps or thin cord to the bottom side of the strips along one end, leaving ½"-1" wide gaps between each board. Repeat on the other side of each board with the cord. Now, you have an easy-to-roll portable walkway!

Never, ever cook inside of your tent, as the scent of food will permeate the entire tent, attracting hungry animals even when there is no food in the tent on future trips.

For foul weather cooking, have a canopy with sides to block the wind. Choose an easy to set up model, and don't forget to use the guy ropes when setting it up, as it greatly enhances the stability of the canopy, especially in rainy weather with gusts of wind. Adding screen sides can keep insects at bay during fair weather, providing shade for both dining and cooking.

Put a piece of old carpet or floor mat in front of the tent door to help keep debris and dirt out of the tent.

Put a camp chair outside your tent door to sit on

while putting shoes on, leaning on while getting in or out of the tent, or holding small items that you don't necessarily want inside the tent with you.

If you have a small freestanding tent, empty the tent first thing in the morning, before cooking breakfast, etc. Tip the tent upside down in a sunny spot to dry the floor before packing the tent up.

Stake your tent down, even if it is a freestanding tent. Without the tent stakes to keep things taut and in place, drafts will make the tent colder in cool weather. In rainy weather, your tent is more likely to leak. If gusty winds come up, even with items inside the tent, it can blow over or even blow away, damaging poles and tent fabric.

Always practice setting up a new tent at home before leaving on your camping trip, even if you are an experienced tent camper. Setting up the tent allows you to seal seams, inspect for flaws or damage, and ensure that all parts for the tent are present.

When shopping for a new tent, always read reviews from consumers as well as ratings from outdoor pros. Consider the guarantee, company reputation, customer service, etc. as well. Sometimes, what looks like a bargain may turn out to be a nightmare. One way to find a good bargain is to buy a close out model or last year's model of tent—manufacturers update tents each year with new fabrics, colors, or slight design changes. Close out models and last year's models come with the same guarantees as the new model, but often with a substantial discount.

Pay attention to tents when camping out, you may see something appealing. Besides, it is a great ice breaker to ask another camper about their tent. Find out what they do and don't like about their tent, as well as the brand and model. They may even offer ideas as to where to find the best price on an identical tent.

Let kids, even the very young ones, help set up and take down tents. Give them age and skill appropriate tasks, even if it is just a case of "hold this stake for me". It makes them feel like they are an important part of the camping project and gets them involved.

Kids can also help unload and load to and from camping trips. Give them items to carry appropriate for their size, even if it is just having them carry their own toy to the vehicle. By letting them help when they are young, they will grow up naturally wanting to help.

Tenting Alternatives

Traditional manufactured tents are the portable homes of choice for most campers today. However, they may not be the most traditional of portable housing, nor are they only choices available. Many of these portable homes are a better choice for long term use as a base camp (weeks or months) than the manufactured tents are.

Many alternatives are actually the traditional homes of nomadic and indigenous people around the world, both today and in times gone by. Some of these homes may be a better option for your family for a number of reasons. In addition, they may provide a connection to your ancestor's culture that is important in terms of your family's identity.

Yurts are a round house formed of a lattice panel covered in felt with poles reaching for a center wheel at the tip of the roof. Coming from the high and cold Mongolian plateau, they are heated by a central fire with the smoke exiting through the hole in the center of the roof. Today, modern versions are sold, both in permanent and semi-permanent styles. Yurts are an excellent choice for long term camping in cold climates.

Canvas wall tents have a long history of use among military units. These heavy tents are cumbersome to set up, heavy to pack, and require strong frames to support them. They come in different configurations and historical replicas are also available to mimic tents used in various military campaigns. These tents also can be equipped with stoves for cooking and heating.

Gypsy wagons are not a tent, but they were definitely portable. Designed originally to be pulled by one or two horses, they were often highly decorated. Modern replicas are typically designed to also be towed by a motor vehicle. Entire families would call one of these wagons home. Some models were bow topped with a canvas roof, while others were created with solid wood roofs.

Sheepherder's wagons were designed to house a man all winter as he tended to his flock of sheep. They were made to be towed by a team of horses in the "olden days" and to be towed by a motor vehicle in more modern times. These compact homes on wheels included a wood or coal stove to cook and heat the wagon, but toilet facilities were non-existent. Modern replicas continue to be made today.

Tipis were once made of buffalo hides by the Indians of the Great Plains. Today, they are typically made from canvas, although they are still offered with traditional double walls. Modern versions are sold in several different sizes, along with poles. Traditionally, they were heated by an open fire in the center, with the smoke exiting the tipi through the roof vent in the center. This vent could be opened or closed by manipulating a pole which was attached to a flap at the peak of the roof, which would help to keep out wind and rain while allowing the smoke to vent out of the tipi.

Chuckwagons, while not a proper home, per se, were a portable kitchen and pantry that accompanied cattle drives and round ups to feed the cowboys who were working the cattle. On this wagon, food and water for the people was carried, along with the pots and pans used by the cook. Typically, the cook was a man, and he would sleep under or in the wagon (if there was room) in his bed roll. The cook was the first one up, as it was his job to start the fire, make coffee and breakfast, as well as get water, find firewood or cow chips to cook on, and clean up the dishes. After breakfast, he would also be required to harness the horses used to tow the wagon, and then drive the wagon to the next location for preparing the evening meal. Besides being the chief cook and bottle washer, the cook was often pressed into duty as a make-do doctor and nurse for any cowboy who was sick or injured. Chuckwagons today typically will serve as mobile lunch wagons for dude ranches and trail rides rather than for working cowboys.

Rooftop tents are also available and are essentially a fold-out platform which holds a tent and is located on the roof of the vehicle it is attached to. The tent is accessed by a ladder. This gets the tent off of the ground, eliminating the need to find a flat campsite. It also reduces the potential exposure to snakes and predators, as well as providing a better opportunity to catch a breeze and stay cool.

Tent cots are a combination of tent and cot. They are available in single and double sizes. There is also a model that is mounted on wheels and designed to be towed by a bicycle. These combo units keep the camper off of the ground, which may be very handy in rocky, wet, or bumpy areas with a lot of low vegetation.

Hammocks are another alternative to tents, especially when equipped with a rain fly and mosquito nets. (See Hammocks for more information)

Bivouac sack or shelters, also known as bivy sacks or shelters, are designed for single person use. The sack is essentially a waterproof bag that fits over the sleeping bag and cinches around the user's face. Water and wind proof, it protects the camper from the elements with the exception of their exposed face. Bivy shelters are essentially a hybrid between the bivy sack and a single person tent. These shelters will often use a hoop or pole to make a raised area over the head and feet of the camper, allowing more breathing room and better protection from the elements.

Tarp shelters have a long history of use as well. Tarps can be erected in a variety of configurations, depending on circumstances, climate, and user needs. Typical set ups include a-frame using saplings and rope for set up, or lean-to, using ropes and saplings again. Properly set up, they can provide excellent weather protection while maximizing the use of a fire for heat or natural breezes for cooling.

A simple lean to tarp shelter using ropes and a walking stick for support shelters this cot.

Toys

Bringing toys for the younger set can help keep them entertained in camp. It does not take a lot of toys or even expensive toys to do the job though. Choose toys that encourage imaginative play in the dirt. This little girl is playing with a toy bulldozer and was occupied for over an hour making small piles of dirt and then spreading them out again.

Another popular type of toy is beach toys designed for playing in the sand. Complete with scoops and often including a storage container too, they are ideal for playing on the beach during a swimming excursion.

Avoid high tech and expensive toys for younger children. They are apt to get mislaid or lost, as well as damaged in the outdoor environment. Encourage them to use their imaginations with simple toys and the great outdoors.

Older children and teens may find their iPad, tablet, or handheld game device entertaining. At the same time, parents may find that it inhibits family participation to allow these devices to accompany them on camping trips. Parents will have to use their discretion about whether they are allowed and what restrictions on their use are imposed.

Travel trailers, pop up campers and motorhomes

For some people, their idea of camping includes a travel trailer or pop up camper for a variety of reasons. There are a variety of models to choose from.

Vintage campers are often a restoration project and hobby, as well as a prize that the owners enjoy showing off when finished. Restored to their like-new glory or redone to a modern expression of their glory, they are often quite luxurious and charming.

Teardrop campers are another vintage style making a comeback. Most are homemade, just like the originals were, and are a showpiece of the craftsman's art. Typically, these have a sleeping compartment and a kitchen under the rear hatch. Canopies provide living and dining space. One of this type's best advantages is that they come in sizes small enough for bicycles, motorcycles, and compact cars.

Ultra-light travel trailers are designed to be lighter in weight than the more traditional styles, and are often feature sleek interiors as well.

Standard travel trailers will also often feature pop out sides to expand living and sleeping areas. Larger travel trailers require a heavy vehicle with a bigger engine to tow them safely.

Self-contained trailers have storage tanks for water, gray water, and sewage. They typically will offer a kitchen sink, toilet and shower. Some may also include a generator and 12 volt electric system.

Self-contained trailers may have either a wet bath or a dry bath. A wet bath is a bathroom with a shower that will drench the entire bathroom, including the toilet. It is as though the toilet is placed in a shower. A dry bath is more like the bathrooms we are accustomed to at home. All RVs and travel trailers use low water use toilets unless they are park models. Park models are ill suited for use by a camper, as they require connection to city water and sewer to function fully.

Motorhomes come in various classes: Class A, B, and C. They package your vehicle and portable home in one convenient package. Each class of motorhome offers different advantages and disadvantages. The larger and more luxurious are found among Class A motorhomes, with price tags to match. Many of these motorhomes offer amenities such as washer/dryer, air conditioning, heat, microwaves, coffee makers, built in surround sound and entertainment systems, and even full sized garden tubs and king size beds.

Purists argue that it is not really camping when traveling with a luxurious travel trailer or motorhome. However, not everyone is willing or able to sleep on a bedroll on the ground. Sometimes, one's spouse is the one refusing to go camping without the conveniences of home as well. Whatever the case may be, anything that encourages people to get out and enjoy nature and our parks is a good thing.

If you are shopping for a travel trailer, camper, pop up camper, or motorhome, looking at many models will help you decide what is and what is not important to you. Knowing what you want will help to make the decision about what kind of camping unit would work best for your family.

Visit an RV show to see many models in a single day.

Often, related products are also being demonstrated at RV shows too.

Pop up campers are a hybrid of tent and travel trailer, hopefully combining the best of both worlds. These campers collapse to provide less wind resistance while traveling, and then are opened up in the campground. Beds are typically extended out from the ends and have windows in their canvas or nylon walls. Typical units have a sink, stove, and dinette. Some units also have air conditioning, built in iceboxes or refrigerators, and heat. Some models also have a bathroom or a potty closet to hold a portable toilet.

In addition to these campers, there are also pickup campers. These campers slide into the bed of a pickup truck, with a bed typically located over the cab of the truck. Most offer a sink, stove, and refrigerator or icebox as well as a dinette that converts to a bed. Since these campers will fit into a four wheel drive pickup, they are often preferred by those who camp in remote locations.

Treats and Snacks

Treats and snacks can make a good camping trip into a great camping trip. A piece of candy or chocolate after a rough hike can be a real morale booster.

Surprise your family on a remote camping trip by bringing along ice cream. Use dry ice inside of a Styrofoam cooler to keep it frozen for several days by taping the lid down.

Make a "cake" by using a package of muffin mix (any flavor) that makes 6 muffins. Mix it according to package directions and pour batter into a greased coffee can. Cover with foil or waxed paper and tie around the can with a piece of twine or cord. Place inside of a covered pot with boiling water reaching up about 1/3 of the can's height. Cover and steam for 30 minutes. Remove can from the water, and cool for 5 minutes before turning can upside down and tapping the cake out of the can onto a plate. Slice and enjoy warm with a cup of coffee or cocoa for a great treat!

Put smiles on everyone's faces with peach fritters.

Simply open a can of peaches and insert a knife, running it through the peaches randomly to cut them up in the can. Pour peaches into a bowl, with the juices, and add enough Krusteaz complete pancake mix (other brands don't seem to work as well) to make a thick batter. Drop by the spoonful into hot oil (2-3" deep in saucepan) and cook until golden brown, draining on a paper bag or paper towels. Sprinkle with sugar, if desired.

© G Miller 2014

Prepackaged single serving baked goods are a great treat that stays fresh through the entire trip.

GORP is a long tradition for snacking while hiking. It stands for Good Old Raisins & Peanuts. Make your own by mixing nuts with dried fruit or even adding extras such as wasabi peas or pretzels for variety.

Vehicles

Car camping means that some kind of vehicle gets you to your campsite. Since most of us don't have a special vehicle dedicated to camping, here are the hacks to help it return to a more civilized state after its camping expedition.

Car top carriers are a great place to pack the first things needed at your campsite, such as your tent, sleeping bags, sleeping pads, etc. Make sure they are packed in waterproof container or securely wrapped in a tarp to keep them dry.

Bicycles can come along for the trip by using a bike carrier. Carriers are available that attach to a receiver hitch, rooftop rack, or are temporarily attached to your trunk or hatchback. Most carry 3-4 bicycles. Adaptors are also available to use on women's bicycles to allow them to easily be carried on these racks.

If towing a trailer of any kind, check lights several days in advance, replacing bulbs as necessary. Check lights again before departing with trailer in tow.

Make it a habit to remove all trash at each stop along the way, whether it is at a rest area or a gas station. This means less trash is lurking in your car when you arrive at your destination or at home.

Check fluids before leaving home, and again before leaving to return home. A quart of oil costs a lot less than a major engine repair!

Check all tires in advance of your camping trip to ensure that they are properly inflated and not excessively worn or damaged.

For less mess while driving, don't eat in the car. Take a break, even if you are picnicking in a rest area, and eat outside the car. It's good for everyone to get out and move around.

Drink only sugar free drinks or water in the car. Sugar makes for sticky messes that are harder to clean up.

Replace windshield wiper blades. New blades mean better visibility in rain and will help keep everyone safe.

Water

We all need water to drink, as well as to do everything from washing our dishes to keeping clean ourselves. While this is not a big problem in a campground with a water spigot at the campsite, it can become a problem if there is no water nearby or in dry camps. Invest in reusable plastic jugs for water. Collapsible containers pack neatly, but are prone to leaking. On average, without taking a shower, each person will use and drink about two gallons of water per day.

Don't use dish soap when washing dishes in a dry camp. Yes, you may have a slight greasy film on the dishes, but it won't kill you. Your water can then be used to give Fido or Fluffy a drink.

Instead of buying water in individual bottles, bring along a re-usable water bottle. Refill from a faucet or bulk container of water and reduce your carbon footprint.

Keep water bottles straight by using a different

color for each family member.

Customize kids' water bottles by adding colorful stickers featuring their favorite cartoon characters. It may even encourage them to drink more water and ask for less soda pop!

Hate odd tasting water? Try the sugar free water flavorings! They are available in a wide variety of flavors from numerous companies and help a lot to hide odd tasting water.

Wildlife

Wild animals should be observed from a distance, never up close. Animals that allow humans to approach are behaving in an unnatural manner and may indicate a sick animal. Many diseases that affect animals can be transmitted to humans. Avoid contact of any kind with an animal that is behaving oddly, and report it to the park ranger as soon as possible.

Do not feed the wildlife. That includes accidental feeding by dropping food in the campsite, on the trail, or leaving a trash can with an unsecured lid. The food we eat is not their natural diet and is apt to make them sick.

Take photos and use the magnifying feature found on most point-and-shoot cameras for a closer look at wildlife. It's a great trophy to collect!

Take advantage of park rangers' knowledge. Attend any programs about the wildlife in the park, ask questions, and view any displays that may be available in the park office or museum.

In bear country, do not cook strong smelling foods. Do not store or prepare food in your tent. Store food securely out of reach of bears as well, remembering that many vehicles have been destroyed by bears in their attempts to gain access to food.

Pick up a guide book about birds of the region and see how many of the local birds you can identify. It's fun, as well as educational.

About the Author

Gia Scott has camped her entire life, and has tried many styles of camping, including minimalism as well as excessive gear. She has spent a great deal of time camping with children, as well as with multi-family camp outs. Gia has also served as camp cook and prepared thousands of meals, both delicious and what was deemed as failed experiments. Much of her camping has also included lessons on foraging and survival tactics, as well as learning about native flora in a variety of locations and climates.

Over the years, she has accompanied many novices into the more natural world, sometimes in campgrounds and sometimes in remote locations. So far, everyone who has ever ventured into the wilds with her has returned home, none the worse for wear. She has also gathered rave reviews from anyone fortunate enough to have joined a camp out when Gia has been the camp cook.

Today, Gia is a grandmother and lives in

Mississippi in a funny little house surrounded by gnarly old live oak trees. There, she writes from her desk or the kitchen table.

Besides this book, Gia has written a dystopian novel titled <u>The Time of Chaos</u>. She has also written a collection of unexplained stories from real life titled <u>Freak Files: The Unexplained Tales</u>. In addition, she has written a common sense handbook for emergency preparation, <u>Being Prepared Without Being A Kook</u>, as well as a book about camping with kids titled <u>Camping With Kids: A Parent's Handbook</u>.

Gia has also written a number of cookbooks, listed here:

- All Chocolate: Easy & Economical Recipes Anyone Can Make At Home
- 55 Fantastic Fudges
- All American Biscuit
- 56+ Marvelous Homemade Mixes
- 55 Frightfully Fun Foods
- At Grandma's Stove

- The Poverty Perspective Cookbook
- 32 Small Breads
- A Home Style Thanksgiving
- Fruitcake!
- My Precious Cookbook
- Sweet Treats: Easy Home Candies
- Dips and Spreads
- No Naked Nachos
- Easy Breezy Family Camping Cookbook
- The Big Book of Camp Cooking

All of Gia's books can be found at www.amazon.com and are available in both print and Kindle.

She always loves to hear from readers, and will sincerely attempt to respond to questions and comments about the books she has written.

Gia can be emailed at giascott@exogenynetwork.com She also appreciates each and every reader, and hopes that they have found each book worthy of being on their book shelf.

Links

Gia's other books can be found at Amazon.com.

Gia's general blog is found at

www.giascott.wordpress.com.

Gia's food blog is found at

www.gulfcoastfoods.wordpress.com.

Gia's camping blog is found at

www.getreadygo.wordpress.com.

Her author page on Facebook is found at

www.facebook.com/giascottblogs